Officer J.J. Popp

K9 Karson Comes Home

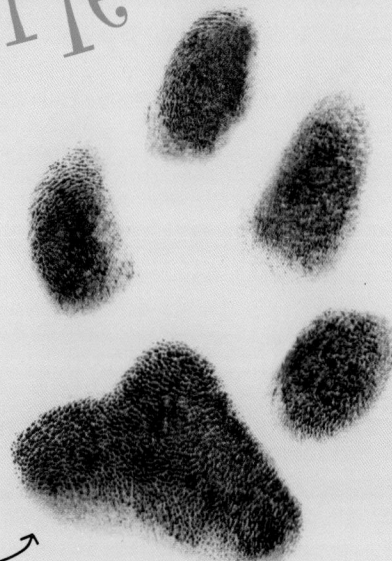

↳ Karson's actual
paw print!

Published for the City of Wilmington by:

Orange Frazer Press

P.O. Box 214

Wilmington, OH 45177

Telephone: 937.382.3196 for price and shipping information.

Website: www.orangefrazer.com

Book and cover design: Alyson Rua and Orange Frazer Press

Library of Congress Control Number: 2015942943

Printed in the United States

June 2015   54060-0   First Edition

Photos on pages 8, 9, 16, 17, 18, 19, 20, and 21 courtesy of Pam Jones

Photos on pages 22 and 23 courtesy of Detective Josh Riley

Photos on pages 12, 13, 26, 27, 28, and 29 courtesy of James B. Gumley

All other photographs courtesy of Officer Jerry Popp and Orange Frazer Press

All proceeds from the sale of this book support the Wilmington Police K-9 program.

K9 Karson Comes Home

Abbie Beam

ORANGE *frazer* PRESS
Wilmington, Ohio

In law enforcement, we're rarely part of an event that brings a community together. However, in December of 2014 we had that happen with the disappearance of K9 Officer Karson. It was the start of a sixty-one-day odyssey when citizens, officers, and dispatchers banded together for a common good. It was wonderful to see the outpouring of support for a noble cause. I was amazed how people would walk trails for hours every day. It was inspiring and heartwarming.

The experience was magnified tenfold when we celebrated Karson's homecoming. Citizens came from everywhere to show their support. The homecoming only lasted two hours and I could barely find the time to thank everyone involved.

This book is dedicated to Officer Popp and his son, Darren, for their unwavering desire to bring Karson home; to the fine officers and communication officers of the Wilmington City Police Department; to the Karson Community (now worldwide) for their resolute support and assistance; and to the citizens of Wilmington, Ohio, for whom we serve.

—Chief Duane Weyand
City of Wilmington Police Department

This book is dedicated to my son, Darren, who drove me to never give up my search; to Jordina Thorp who taught me that quitting is never an option and that even the darkest nights hold hope; and to the tens of thousands of friends, followers, and fans of Karson who relentlessly believed that in the spirit of faith, together we could accomplish anything.

—Officer Jerry Popp
City of Wilmington Police Department

K9 Karson Comes Home

Meet K9 Karson!

Karson the dog is a three-year-old Belgian Malinois. He became an officer for the Wilmington, Ohio, Police Department in 2013. He is trained to sniff out drugs, to track humans, and to assist in catching criminals.

On December 23, 2014, while Officer Popp was gone, Karson was being cared for by others. Karson missed Officer Popp so much that he ran away to find him.

Karson ran and ran trying to find Officer Popp whose home was in another county. It was very cold and snowy. The temperatures were below zero degrees. Karson had to use his survival skills to stay alive.

cold and snowy

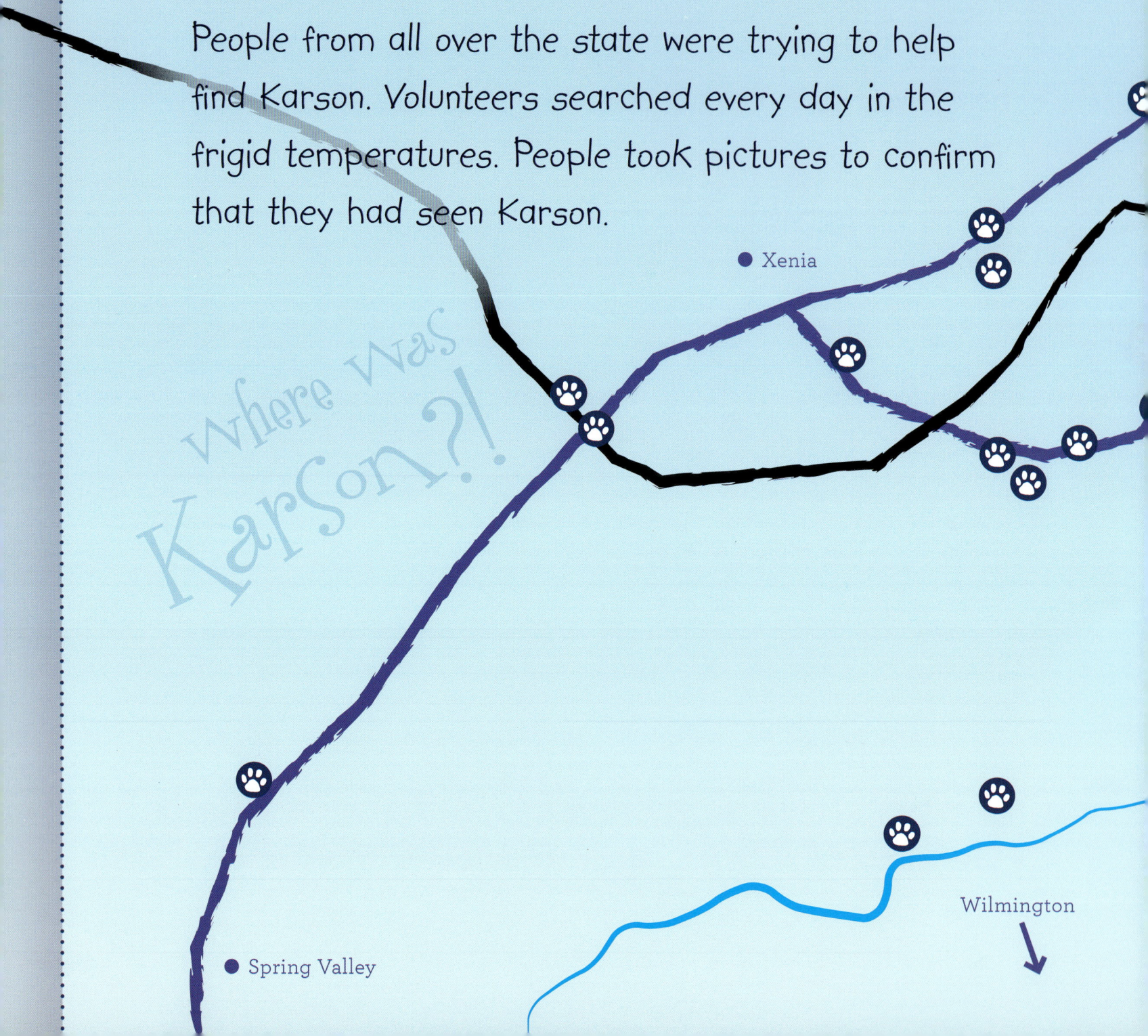

People from all over the state were trying to help find Karson. Volunteers searched every day in the frigid temperatures. People took pictures to confirm that they had seen Karson.

Where was Karson?!

Wilberforce

Xenia

Spring Valley

Wilmington

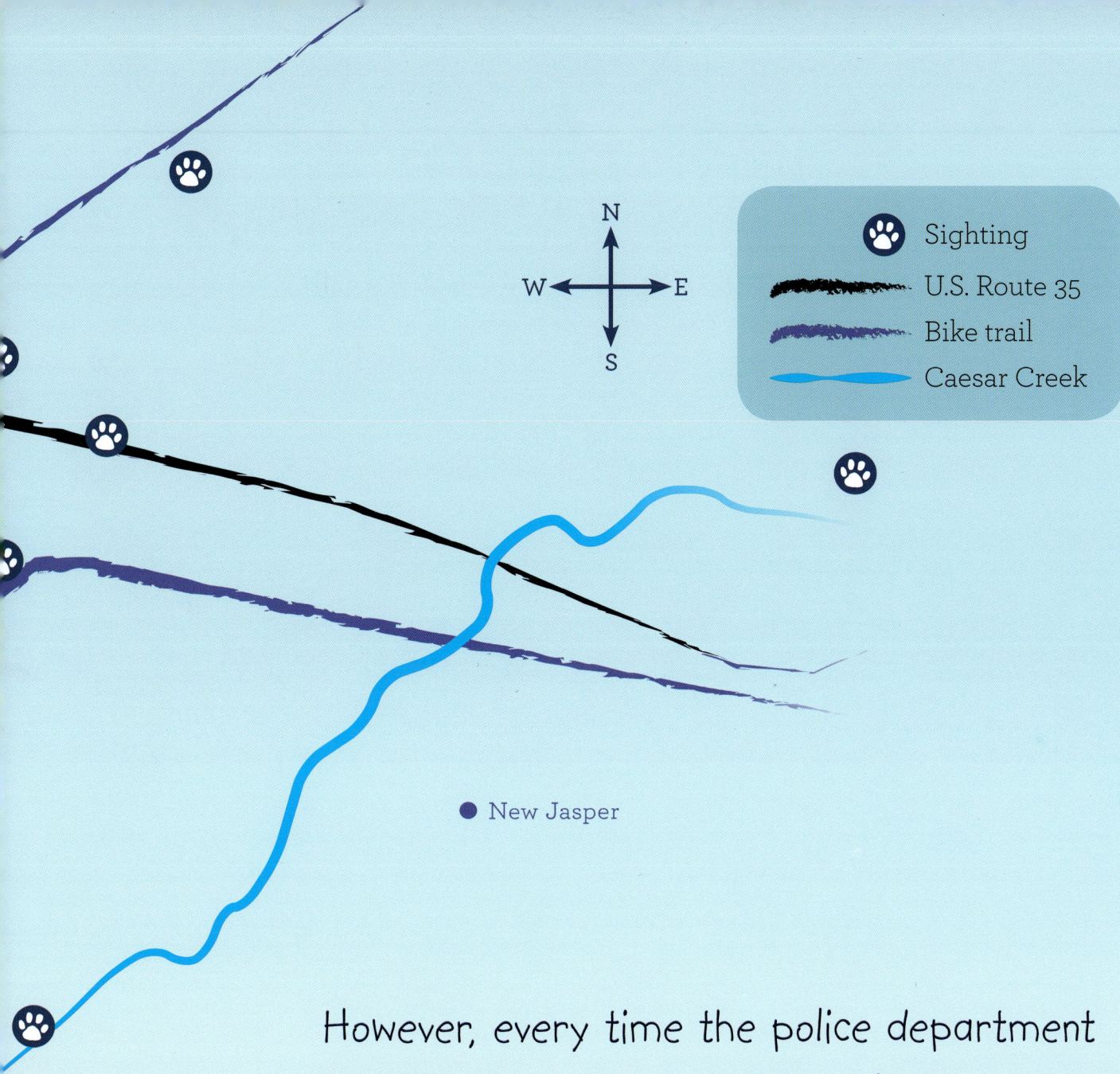

Legend

🐾	Sighting
▬▬▬	U.S. Route 35
▬▬▬	Bike trail
〰〰	Caesar Creek

● New Jasper

However, every time the police department received the news and Officer Popp reached the location, Karson would be gone.

Word spread across the land. People from all over the United States and Canada sent cards and well wishes to Officer Popp and Karson, hoping for a safe return.

Over 30,000 people were following Karson's story on Facebook. TV stations and newspapers were covering Karson's story. Flyers were posted in businesses and on telephone poles. It seemed that everyone was looking for Karson!

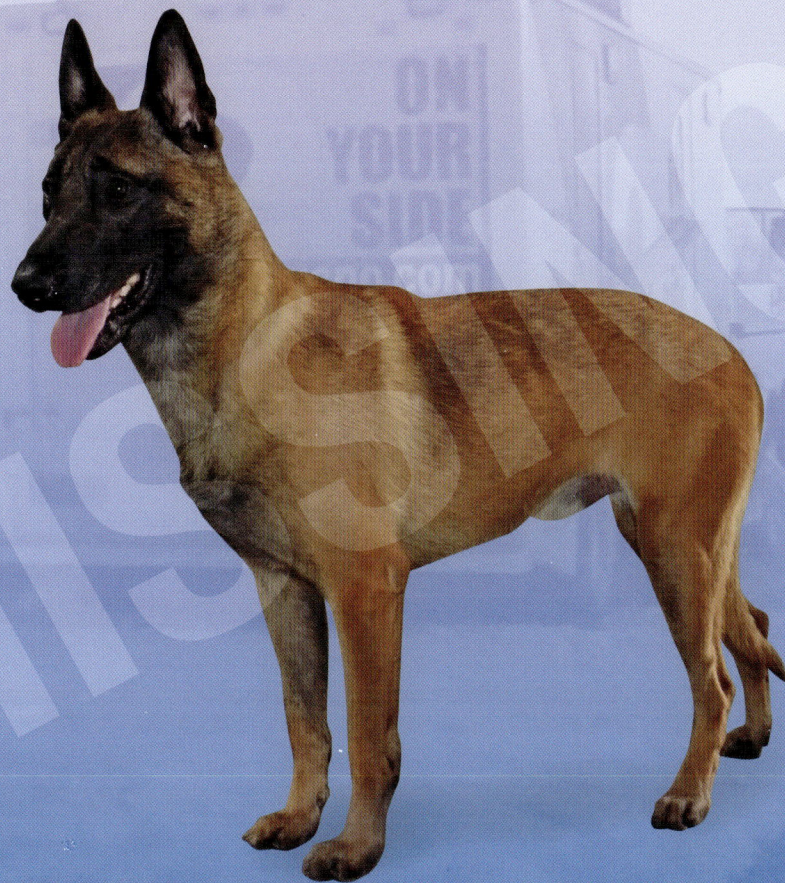

Karson loves tennis balls, so people started giving Officer Popp tennis balls for when Karson came home.

paws crossed

Other people drove around looking for Karson and kept tennis balls in their cars. People started posting, "Paws crossed and tennis ball on dash," as a sign they would not give up on Karson.

Around noon on February 22, the last day of the official two-month search, a miracle happened! A husband and wife from Mason, Ohio, were driving on the highway towards Columbus and spotted Karson in an open field. They flagged down an officer and pointed to Karson. The wife, a professional photographer, took pictures which confirmed that the dog was indeed Karson!

miracle!

It is thought that during the last few days Karson had been living in a hog barn in that field, drinking water from a stream, and living off of the land. Neighbors had seen what they thought was a coyote in the same area, but now know that it was Karson!

1/800   8.0   100-6966 CF

15/17

Canon

Sheriff deputies, police officers, and the Ohio State Highway Patrol showed up to help catch Karson. Karson was in an open field and they were able to surround him so he could not get away. Sergeant Fithen, Wilmington's first K9 handler, was in a police truck. He drove into the field to follow Karson until Karson got tired and stopped running.

Karson was safe

Officer Popp was on foot trying to reach Karson. Sergeant Fithen called Karson's name. Karson looked at him. Sergeant Fithen got out of the truck, opened the door, and squatted down to look less scary. The command was given to get in the truck. Karson jumped in. The door was closed and Karson was safe!

tears of joy

Officer Popp was very, very tired from the sixty-one-day search for his K9 partner. He fell to the ground and gave thanks. There were tears of joy from everyone!

Officer Popp got into the police truck where Karson was waiting. This was the moment everyone had been waiting to see. You could see the love and relief as Officer Popp sat with his K9 partner.

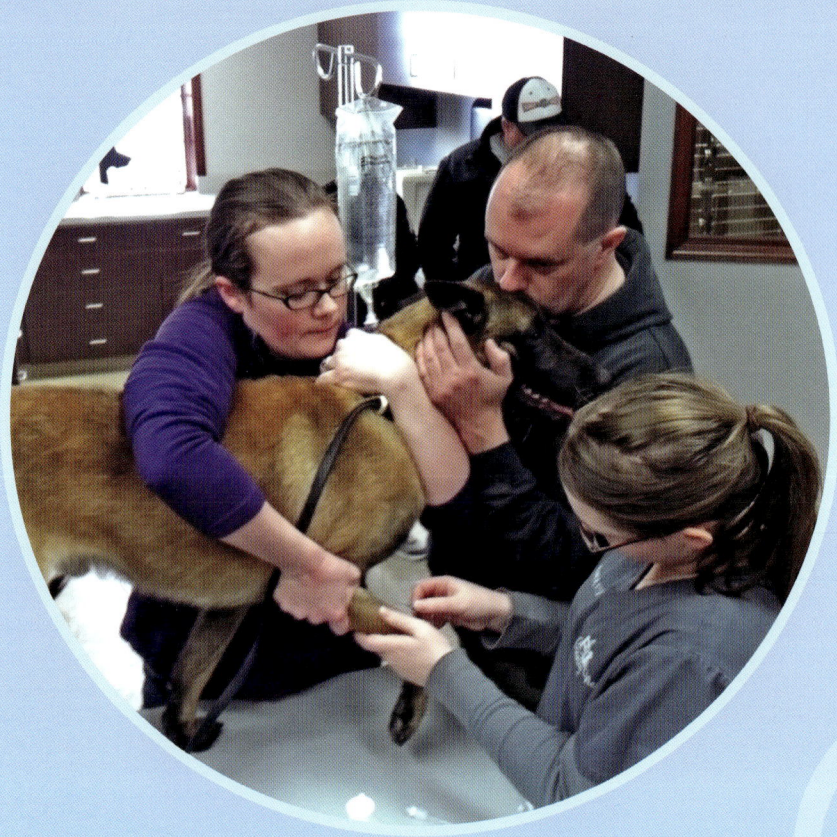

Karson was taken to a local veterinary clinic to be checked out. Even though Karson had been out in the cold for sixty-one days, his health was good. It is thought that Karson traveled over 200 miles trying to find his way home.

His paws were red, he had lost fourteen pounds, and he was very thirsty. He had even been sprayed by a skunk! Karson was given some medicine and then went home with Officer Popp.

When Karson got home he was exhausted. Later that evening Karson played with his tennis ball. When Officer Popp went to the garage, Karson went with him. Karson walked up to the K9 cruiser and sat by the door until Officer Popp opened it. Karson jumped in. This was Karson's way of telling Officer Popp that he was still his K9 partner.

Officer Popp was told that Karson would get back into his routine once he came home, and he did. That first evening he was responding to basic commands. Karson slept through the night on his bed next to Officer Popp.

through
the night

On February 27, the community hosted a Welcome Home Ceremony for Karson. Nine hundred people arrived to meet Officer Popp and Karson! By the time Karson had greeted them all, he was so tired that he lay down and fell asleep next to Officer Popp.

hope
and love

It was a wonderful ending to a story about perseverance, loyalty, hope, and love. No one gave up! Everyone came together to be a part of this amazing story.

K9 Karson is now recertified and is back on duty alongside Officer Popp, helping to keep our community safe.

🐾 A Special Thanks

Pam Jones and her husband, Rick, were headed north on I-71 towards Columbus to do a photo shoot. They saw what they thought might be Karson running in a field. Pam got her camera out and took pictures. As Pam looked at the pictures, she was certain that it was Karson. They called 911 and flagged down a sheriff's deputy and showed him the images. The deputy yelled Karson's name and Karson stopped and looked at him. The rest is history with a great ending.

Pam has been a professional photographer from Mason, Ohio, for fifteen years. She feels blessed that she was at the right place at the right time with her camera. Pam's immediate thought was to document through pictures what was taking place. These images were shared immediately on K9 Karson's Facebook page allowing Karson's community of followers to feel as though they were witnessing the rescue as it happened.

As a published photographer, locating and documenting Karson's capture has been one of her greatest career highlights.

🐾 About the Author

Born and raised at the edge of Wilmington, Ohio, Abbie Arnold Beam enjoyed a wonderful childhood. As an only child, she spent a lot of time with her friends, cousins, and menagerie of animals. Her mother was an educator and her father was a businessman. Reading was instilled in her from an early age. One of her cherished childhood memories is of sitting under a tree and reading to her animals.

Abbie's love of books continued and she became a teacher. She graduated from Wilmington High School in 1981 and later from Wilmington College in 1983 with degrees in K-12 Special Education, K-8 Regular Education, and Gifted Education. She received her Masters Degree in Education from Miami University in 1986. Abbie taught students with special needs and had therapy dogs in her classroom.

Abbie lives near Wilmington with her husband. They have a daughter, a son, and several pets. Abbie recently retired from teaching, which allowed her the opportunity to pursue her dream of writing.

Visit K9 Karson on his very own Facebook
page, **K9 Karson**, where thousands of fans follow
his latest news!